EVERY WOMAN'S GUIDE TO CAREER SUCCESS

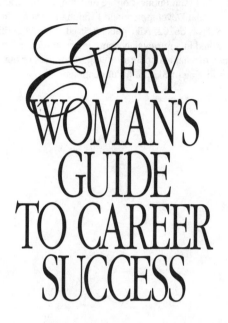

EVERY WOMAN'S GUIDE TO CAREER SUCCESS

Denise M. Dudley

SkillPath Publications
Mission, Kansas

Copy Editor
Kelly Scanlon

Creative Assistant
Virginia Crabtree

Cover Design
Rod Hankins

Library of Congress Catalog Card Number: 95-71725

ISBN: 1-878542-25-7

10   9   8   7   6   5   99   00

Printed in the United States of America

One can never consent to creep, when one feels an impulse to soar.
—Helen Keller

Corporate affirmative action provides an important function, but it is no substitute for personal affirmative action. Personal affirmative action—a concerted effort to succeed using all the self-help tools at your disposal—is the only real solution for women who want to advance in their careers.
—from the book *Upward Mobility*
published by Catalyst*

*Catalyst is a national nonprofit organization dedicated to expanding career and family options for women. For more information, write them at 250 Park Avenue South, New York, NY 10003.

CONTENTS

PREFACE

Dear Friend,

If you're like most of us, sometimes the view you get of the top from your rung on the Ladder of Success makes you dizzy. You've heard some things about what it's supposed to take to get ahead in your career, and you wonder where they're issuing the superwoman underwear. You're frustrated and overwhelmed by what appears to be an impossible—or at least backbreaking—climb to success.

Do you aspire to a position higher than the one you now have? Could your income stand to be doubled? Have you decided you want to make moving up in your career a priority, but find yourself confused by the mountain of information available on the subject? Do you want to enjoy your life while you are working at getting ahead? Yes?

Then this book is for you.

Libraries, bookstores, and many women's shelves are filled to overflowing with books telling you how to get ahead in your career. They are loaded with all kinds of advice, ranging from "Eat the right foods and wear conservative makeup" to "Analyze the success potential of your organization and position yourself for growth." Which advice should you follow? How can you tell what will work in your life, in your particular situation?

Dr. Benjamin Spock begins his book *Dr. Spock's Baby and Child Care* with a chapter titled "Trust Yourself." Its first sentence is "You know more than you think you do."[1]

1. Benjamin Spock, *Baby and Child Care (rev. ed.)* (New York: Hawthorn Books, 1976), 1.

Before her daughter was born, Maria thought Spock was crazy. How could she trust herself with all those important details, like teaching her daughter how to eat, how to talk, and how to walk? She didn't know that those things just take care of themselves. Once she figured that out, childrearing became much easier. Maria used Dr. Spock's book as reassurance that the things she did were OK and that the things she didn't do were OK not to do.

What Dr. Spock says to parents about their children is also good advice for women contemplating their careers: You know more than you think. You know more about your job, your boss, your co-workers, your family, your hopes, and your dreams than anyone else.

This book is meant to give you lots of support, some breaths of fresh air, and, occasionally, an answer you may never have considered before. Some of the ideas presented here will grab you immediately, and others may not appeal to you strongly. Trust yourself. Two of the most common qualities you'll find in successful women (or men) is their self-assurance and willingness to trust their instincts.

This book covers five major areas: education and training, professional image, management savvy, public relations, and personal power. Among them, they discuss all the major techniques you can use to achieve career success. Beyond that, the only thing you need to know is that *Every Woman's Guide to Career Success* is a handbook. It lists simple suggestions with short explanations pertaining to each of the main areas. Browse through those suggestions and find some that seem particularly appropriate to your needs. Or just let the book fall open and read the first few you see.

Whatever you do, don't beat yourself to death with this book: "Oh, look, I'm supposed to be controlling my emotions at the office, going to school, saying no to my boss, going to conventions, and not smoking! I can't go through with it!" Well, at that pace, of course you can't.

Pick just five ideas to try in the next thirty days. If you practice them, I guarantee you will be well on your way to professional success. How do I know that? Because by taking action, you actually take the helm and steer your ship in the direction you choose for it, instead of letting it drift with the wind and the tide. You control your destiny, and even if an unexpected storm comes, you will have the conviction that you are doing everything you can to get where you want to go.

So, good luck to you on your journey. Enjoy this book. Let it work for you.

Sincerely,

EDUCATION AND TRAINING

To keep a lamp burning we have to keep putting oil in it.
– Mother Teresa

He not busy being born is busy dying.
– Bob Dylan

I am still learning.
– Michelangelo's motto

Formal education, company-sponsored training programs, public seminars—even your own independent study—can help you advance in your career. The enthusiasm you have for your own growth is contagious; you will become known as a willing and capable employee, and you will be getting smarter by the minute to boot.

Of course, it should go without saying that sometimes your career goals demand that you seek certain education or training. If you want to be a lawyer, you'll need to graduate from law school. If you intend to advance to the position of director of information services for your company, you'll definitely need to learn as much as you can about the company's computer system—and most likely, a lot about the company itself. By all means, get the education or training you need—and more.

Get Training

"Training" is the business world's word for education. Company-sponsored training classes or public seminars increase your knowledge and improve your visibility. Usually your company will pay for these.

Tell your boss about Debbi Fields' Cookie College. Cookie College is a 10-day course designed to communicate the company's expectations to new recruits, teach corporate values, develop skills, and identify promotable people. Every Mrs. Fields' employee goes to the company's Utah headquarters and participates in the training. Even the newest employee is treated as a career professional, not as a dough maker paid by the hour. Here's the important part to impress your boss with: When Cookie College began, Mrs. Fields' employee turnover was *halved.* And here's the important lesson for you: *Promotable people are spotted more quickly inside a corporate classroom than outside one.*

Even if your company won't pay for you to attend, it's a good idea to make the commitment to send yourself to a business skills seminar at least once every six months. (Most one-day seminars cost under $100—and many are under $60.) Make sure you are on at least one mailing list to receive seminar schedules for your city. Pick a topic that will advance you toward your career goal—training, writing skills, presentation skills, assertiveness training. The list of available seminars is practically endless. Besides providing a way for you to learn some new skills regularly, this commitment will ensure that you get out and meet your peers. Seminars are a great place to start your own support network.

Get Sales Training

Sales experience is good for anyone—and it's especially important for women trying to get ahead in what is still, in many ways, a man's world. Many people still see women only as homemakers and mothers, not as directors of marketing for Fortune 500 corporations. As women, we must overcome these limiting stereotypes, in short, by selling ourselves as the professionals we know we are or that we aspire to become.

Most jobs have more to do with selling than we suspect. Even the most insular of jobs involves marketing. A librarian, for example, needs to sell the joy of reading to the community. If she doesn't, and the circulation numbers go down, the library may lose funding. A secretary needs the ability to sell her work and her image to her employer. If you think you don't need sales skills, think again. Not many careers grow in a vacuum. If you need to influence other people, you need to know how to sell.

The qualities that make for a truly successful sales ability are those that you can always improve. Salespeople are not the high-pressure, say anything-you-want-to-hear types selling used cars to little old ladies and rhinestone jewelry to lonely hearts at home watching TV. Today's successful marketers are sincerely committed to the products or ideas they sell. They are enthusiastic and, more important, they generate that enthusiasm in others.

Get More Formal Education

Go back to school. There are colleges and universities just about everywhere, and many companies have tuition reimbursement plans to help you. Or, if you—like many working women—just don't have the time for formal classes, get in touch with the National University Continuing Education Association (NUCEA) and ask for its directory of off-campus degree programs. (The address is 1 Dupont Circle, Suite 420, Washington, DC 20036.) There are at least 100 colleges and universities that offer correspondence courses, credit by examination, and independent study opportunities to students who want a degree but cannot commit to class time.

Become Computer Literate—Now

A 1988 article in *Working Woman* magazine asked four of the most successful women in management and technology to share their insights on how technology would affect the world of work in the 1990s.[1] Even then everyone seemed to agree that computers had become as much a part of every office environment as telephones.

The 1980s brought us to terms with this new machine, the personal computer. In the 1990s the PC is widespread and capable enough that using it is a matter of course. If you can't already compute your way out of a wet paper bag, you'd better learn—soon. To *have* a future, you must be *part* of that future.

If you are already an expert with your PC, build on that foundation. Keep abreast of new developments, particularly in software.

Five years ago, Andrea was hired to manage the office of a progressive consulting firm. She had never worked on a PC, so the company trained her to use the most popular word processing package it could find—WordStar. A motivated employee, Andrea quickly became fluent in the software and earned the reputation as the company's WordStar expert. Subsequently, however, Andrea's company announced plans to relocate. Andrea did not want to move, so she began to search for another job. She was shocked to learn that no one she interviewed with cared much about her WordStar experience; everyone wanted WordPerfect.

As you will read many times in this book, to have the kind of career success that you want, you must remain teachable.

Understand What's Expected

Follow your job description. If you don't have one, each morning ask your boss what you should set as your five most important priorities for the day. The few minutes you spend educating yourself about your boss's expectations will pay handsomely. Your boss will view you as a dedicated employee, and you will be equipped with the information you need to do what you're being paid to do. In fact, review your own performance at the end of each day by asking yourself, "Did I accomplish what I'm paid to do today?"

About that job description—if you don't have one, start keeping a list of the things you do at work. Such a list will be useful when you are being reviewed, apply for a promotion, or need to write a résumé. You can also use the list to write a job description yourself and then ask your boss if it's accurate.

Learn About Your Workplace

In an interview with *Training* magazine, Jack E. Bowsher, the director of education for external programs for IBM, said: "This is the advice I give to anybody in any career. You have to become an expert. People have to look at you and say that you know more about this than anybody else."[2]

Do your homework. Are you the mail sorter for your organization? Don't just sort the mail, *look* at it. Learn about your organization and the work it does. Who are its competitors?

Imagine you are the accounts receivable manager for the Ace Peabo Corporation. Do you know what a peabo is? Who else makes them? Why are your company's peabos superior to all others? It probably wouldn't hurt to glance occasionally at an issue of the professional journal *Peabos Today*. And if you read an article *anywhere* about your organization's business, be sure to call it to someone's attention.

Learn the language of your business. Try to understand how the department in which you work fits into the structure of the whole organization.

Find a Mentor

Having a mentor is one of the fastest and surest ways to move forward professionally. Unfortunately, you can't generally go out and find a mentor; mentors find you. But you can recognize when you're being chosen and nurture the relationship.

In her book *Breaking the Secretary Barrier*, Janet Dight contends that often when managers try to be mentors, they are rebuffed (usually unintentionally) by the people they are trying to help. According to Dight, here are four signs that indicate you are being chosen by a mentor:

1. Mentors share their pasts with you.

2. Mentors are willing to spend extra time and effort helping you.

3. Mentors try to get you better assignments.

4. Mentors are genuinely interested in the future of your career.[3]

To ensure a smooth and lasting relationship with your mentor, Dight advises:

1. Don't confuse professional interest with personal interest. Although your mentor generally is more than willing to help you improve your professional standing, do not assume that she or he is interested in mending personal relationships or becoming involved with you socially. Keep the relationship on a business level.

2. Don't flaunt the relationship. You risk offending your mentor if you brag.

3. Don't let your mentor down. Live up to her or his expectations. A mentor gives you one of the best opportunities you'll ever have for getting ahead. Don't let either of you down.[4]

Learn to Pick Brains

With or without a mentor, be ready to gain as much knowledge as you can through the contacts you make on behalf of your organization. For example, if your company publishes books and the printer's representative frequently visits your office, take a moment to greet that person. Ask a couple of questions about the printing business, especially as it relates to your company.

Subscribe to a Professional Publication

Reading professional or trade publications is a great way to learn about your organization's business. You don't need to read every issue of every journal or magazine cover to cover; sometimes just glancing through, reading a couple of articles, is enough to keep you in step with what's happening in your profession.

Here's another tip for keeping current: Subscribe to a magazine just for women. Whether it's *Working Woman*, *Vogue*, *Savvy*, *Working Mother*, or *Good Housekeeping*, pick one that you genuinely enjoy.

Use Your Downtime Constructively

Most people spend nearly an hour a day commuting to and from work. If you drive, use that time productively by listening to audiocassette programs. Many excellent titles are available on just about any subject: prosperity, self-esteem, relationships, assertiveness, and writing skills to name a few. Tape sets are available from many public libraries, bookstores, and seminar companies. There are also several companies that specialize in producing and marketing educational audiocassettes. One of the most well known is Nightingale-Conant Corporation. Write or call the company for a catalog: 7300 North Lehigh Avenue, Chicago, IL 60648; (312) 647-0300.

If you use public transportation, you have even more options available. You can listen to tapes if you invest in an inexpensive portable tape player with earphones. If you prefer reading, this would be a good time to pull out the latest issue of a professional journal. Or, make a point of reading some of the thousands of good books available on a variety of subjects helpful to professional women. (You'll find a bibliography of some of these at the end of this book.)

Don't Stop Learning

Even if it's just reading a self-help book you picked up at the bookstore or listening to an audiocassette program on your way to and from work, *always keep your education active at some level or another*. The effort will refresh you—kind of like a brisk walk around the block every morning—and keep you growing personally and professionally. Keep challenging yourself. What new thing are you trying these days? It's common knowledge that people who keep themselves fresh stand pretty good chances of living the lives they dream of. Commit to it!

Endnotes

1. John Stoltenberg, "Turning Problems Into Profits," *Working Woman* 13(5) (May 1988): 63.

2. Beverly Geber, "Six-Figure Trainers," *Training: The Magazine of Human Resource Development* 25 (November 1988): 44.

3. Janet Dight, *Breaking the Secretary Barrier* (New York: McGraw-Hill, 1988), 266.

4. Ibid., 267.

PROFESSIONAL IMAGE

A rock pile ceases to be a rock pile the moment a single man contemplates it, bearing within him the image of a cathedral.
— Antoine de Saint Exupery

Whatever the mind of a man can conceive and believe it can achieve.
— Napoleon Hill

"Tell me, Miss Taggart, what's going to support a seven-thousand-ton train on a three-thousand-ton bridge?"

"My judgment," she answered.
— from *Atlas Shrugged*, by Ayn Rand

If you treat yourself as a professional, you will see yourself as one. And if you see yourself as a professional, it will be more natural for you to act like one. This is the key to the suggestions in this chapter.

Dagny Taggart, the heroine of Ayn Rand's *Atlas Shrugged*, is a role model to keep in mind. She *never* doubts that her judgment is sound, never turns away from reality, and never loses her integrity. She is passionate in her convictions and always ready to *take the action* her judgment and her beliefs dictate.

A professional image is not formed just by the clothes you wear (although clothes are a part of it). It is formed by the way you project yourself to others as a total person. How do you handle pressure? Whom do you associate with? How do you communicate?

This chapter gives you some tips that will improve your professional image. But remember, they have to work for you. Choose a couple that appeal to you and get started. Come back later to consider the others.

Dress Professionally

Dress for the job you want, not the job you have. Dressing in the most professional manner you can not only makes you look good—it makes you feel powerful.

What is the "intimidation suit" of the year? Currently, it is an elegantly cut (not mannish), dark-colored suit with knee-length skirt and a silk blouse. A small amount of good jewelry, a trim shoulder bag, leather briefcase, and closed-toe pump complete the look.

The October 1988 issue of *Working Woman* magazine published the results of a professional image survey it conducted. The survey provides useful information for achieving a professional look.[1] Many other magazines offering advice on dressing professionally are available. Check them out.

The best rule for hair and makeup at work is simple: Notice what the professional women in your office are wearing and try to stay in step. If you are the manager of a contemporary hair salon, the hairstyle and makeup you need are much different than they are for the office manager at the Mother House of the Sisters of the Incarnate Word.

In a nutshell: Fit in. Usually that means wearing a neat hairstyle and some, but not too much, makeup.

A special note for women who travel around the country in their work: Do with your hair, makeup, and clothes what the toothpaste companies have done for years. Ask yourself, "Will this work in Kansas City?" Many new products are tested in Kansas City because it is considered the heart of middle America—and the tests prove accurate. Your safest bet is always the middle ground.

Don't Be an Office Drone

In her book *Getting on Top*, Melody Sharp Quarnstrom says: "You'll never make it up on deck where the air is fresh and the action exhilarating unless you set yourself apart from the rest of the rowers."[2] Her suggestion? Arrive at work a few minutes early occasionally, and never leave at the stroke of five. Stay to finish the job you're working on. While you're there, by the way, notice who else is with you. That's right—the other movers and shakers.

Buy a Time Management System

The appointment book of the 1980s has grown into the time management system of the 1990s. It contains daily and monthly calendars as well as address and phone pages, "to do" lists, project reporting sheets, finance and expense pages, maps, and many other optional sections. Make sure the time management system you use has a section for notes. As you will see in the next few pages, this section is the most important feature.

Even if you only use the book to write down your appointments, contacts, and ideas throughout the day, you'll find it immensely helpful. All the information you need will be in one place.

Joanna, an administrative assistant to the president of her organization, was frustrated with the slow pace of her career development. She was motivated and intelligent, but even the extra hours she put in did nothing to change her status. On an impulse, she bought a Day Runner Entrepreneur. One year later, she was making over $30,000 a year and her title was director of education—for the same company.

The Day Runner may not have been the only reason for Joanna's promotion, but it did wonders for her image as a professional. People who had seen Joanna as an efficient secretary began to take a look at her management potential. Using the Day Runner made Joanna take herself seriously as a well-organized professional. And that meant others saw her that way too.

Take Notes

Most people know what an effective learning tool note taking can be. But taking notes is an effective political tool, too, particularly for a woman on her way to the top.

The first thing note taking can do for your career is put you in control. When you jot things down during a conversation, you put yourself in an active role. You send a message that you not only hear what your coworker is saying, but that you intend to do something about it.

Another benefit of taking notes is that it provides you with a store of personalized information. You can access the details of the project you are working on and instantly see your own involvement and contributions. Questions written in the heat of a conversation become the foundation of new projects. Ideas that may have seemed irrelevant provide a new focus when enthusiasm for a project begins to lose its momentum. Sooner or later, you will become known as a creative person, the person with the answers, or at least the person to kick around the questions with.

Finally, note taking simply helps to keep your mind focused on the task at hand. If a thought unrelated to work crosses your mind, you have a choice. Do you let it stay there and ruin your concentration? Or do you jot it down for later reference and keep plugging away?

Ignore Negative Energy

The next time someone in the office makes a negative comment, face it with a sense of humor. Here's an example: You have just entered the elevator at 4:15 on Friday afternoon. Another person in the elevator says, "Oh, sneaking out of work early?" The woman who makes a point to ignore negative energy could respond, "Well no, I'm taking a late lunch since I plan to work late tonight."

Make Your Job Look Better Than It Is

Handle even the most lowly chores with a sense of purpose and respect. If you are in charge of ordering supplies for the office, ask the purchasing agent which vendors give the best prices and then spend some time browsing through catalogs until you find the *perfect* legal-size hanging file folders. As you do your job well, your knowledge will expand. Little decisions are still decisions.

Expand Your Lunch Dates

Nurture a few relationships with women in positions higher than yours. One at a time, learn a bit about each woman and what she does. Compliment one on her achievements, and invite her to lunch. Ask her how she got so far so fast.

Control Your Emotions

Especially don't cry or rant. If you have objections, state them calmly and courteously. Never show hostility. Who says? *Everyone* says.

In *Breaking the Secretary Barrier,* Janet Dight presents these suggestions for women seeking to gain emotional control:

1. Diffuse the situation before it escalates. When things go wrong, address the situation as soon as possible.

2. If an emotional confrontation is unavoidable, don't succumb to the "end-of-the-world syndrome." Put the situation in perspective. The world will not end if you make a mistake; ruffled feathers can be smoothed, relationships can be mended.

3. Remember that your response can determine the outcome. The more professionally you respond to a situation in which emotions are running high, the sooner it will be resolved. The more emotionally you react, the worse you make the problem and prolong its resolution.

4. Remember your career goals. Two minutes of screaming can unravel months of strategy designed to put you in line for a promotion.

5. Keep a stiff upper lip. If you've just been reprimanded, passed over for promotion, or handed a bad assignment, hold your head up and smile. Be just as pleasant as you would on a day when things are going well. Show your boss that nothing can make you fold.

6. If, in spite of your best efforts, you think you are going to lose control, leave the room. Apologize and suggest meeting at a later time. Then go somewhere where you can regain your composure.[3]

Use Simple, Active Language

Professor Henry Higgins was right—correct speech gives the impression of intelligence. In fact, experts recommend that you create an image of high productivity by describing your work in simple, active verbs. Avoid the passive voice. Say "I planned your trip," not "Your trip's been planned." And, of course, don't use profane language.

Ask For a New Title

Mary Bridgett Carroll, author of *Overworked and Underpaid,* says that with a new title such as assistant director of sales, you may not make any more money or do anything differently than you do now. But the title can make a big difference, especially if you decide to switch to another company.[4]

Julie worked for a small training company that does a lot of accounting training for automobile manufacturers. As a training specialist, she designed customized programs for the various departments of the companies that used her employer's services.

She felt she could probably find another job doing the same thing for at least $5,000 a year more. But when she asked her boss for a raise, she was denied on the grounds that training specialists were "*all* paid that amount." When she didn't get anywhere with the money issue, she tried something else. She said, "Well, actually, I don't think my title accurately represents my contribution to the company. I am the only person here who customizes our programs." She convinced her boss that her title should be director of client programs.

Six months later she was making $15,000 more a year working for a different company. She was hired because she was the most talented applicant interviewed; it had nothing to do with her title. But she had been interviewed in the first place because her résumé had made it through the first screening. Why? *Her title*.

Don't Blame—Fix the Cause

Blaming is often a natural response when things go wrong. The only drawback is that it doesn't work. Nothing is as refreshing or professional as the ability to get to the heart of a problem and fix it—without bothering to place blame.

How often have you heard this at work: "Well, Martha should have told us we were running out of Number 7 boxes before this! We'll never have enough to fill these orders!"

How often have you heard this: "Ms. Walker, we're going to run out of our Number 7 boxes today. I have placed a rush order for more, and they'll be here next Wednesday. In the meantime, I've instructed Martha to pack all the orders she'd normally pack in a Number 7 in two Number 5s. We have plenty of packing peanuts to fill in the extra space. Is this all right with you?"

Dollars to donuts, Ms. Walker is so thrilled about *not* having to develop the contingency plan herself that *any* workable suggestion will win her favor—as will the professional who suggested it.

Be a Team Player

The ability to work well with others is crucial to your professional success. This is one of the hardest lessons for many women to learn. In part, this is because women are not taught good "team-sport etiquette."

Michelle was raised to be self-sufficient, and she carried it to extremes at her job in field sales. She wanted to show everyone how capable and smart she was. She refused help on projects and didn't bother to get to know her coworkers. She competed with them all the time; the resulting pressure was incredible.

Finally, a kind boss forced her to accept help on a project. He assigned her best friend, Nancy, to the job. Their goal was to organize a raffle for 100 sales representatives. In the raffle, each rep was given the same number of chances as he or she had sales for the month. The top rep had earned 121 chances; the lowest had earned one.

It took Michelle and Nancy a while to organize the project. Finally, they decided to use poker chips as tickets—poker chips with little round labels stuck on them. On the labels, they wrote each rep's four-digit rep code. Michelle and Nancy will never forget the fun they had writing the number "2909" 121 times and then sticking those little labels on the poker chips. The job took at least half the time it would have taken Michelle alone, and it's remained one of the happiest memories of her working life. Most important, it was a small step on the road to being able to work in a team.

Eight years have passed since the poker chip project. Two years ago Michelle represented her company in a meeting with training executives of IBM and one of the Big Three automakers to discuss a possible joint venture between the three organizations. It took six years, but Michelle gradually acquired a reputation for being a good team player.

Be Sensitive to Organizational Politics

Ideas rarely start at the top, but they must look as if they did. If you have a good idea and the position to present it and be heard, go for it. If not, talk it up to someone who can suggest it and be heard. Don't risk offending anyone up the hierarchy by grandstanding.

Join a Professional Association

Joining a professional association is a great tool for making contacts, learning more about your business, and getting ahead in your career. Many of these organizations also offer benefits like car rental discounts, job postings, health insurance, and journal subscriptions. Which association should you join? Your first choice should be the major association of your profession. If you don't know which one that is, ask around. It's likely that someone in your office belongs to it. (It's also likely, by the way, that your company will pay all or part of the membership fee.)

What if you are the manager of support services for a branch office of a huge corporation like IBM or General Motors? Or a training assistant at an accounting firm? Should you join the

International Society of Business Machine Manufacturers, or the American Society of Automakers? Probably not. In those cases, you'd probably be better joining an organization more appropriate to your specific situation.

The National Association for Female Executives, for example, provides members with a subscription to *Executive Female*, a bimonthly magazine providing information on career advancement and financial planning. (The association is located at 127 West 24th Street, New York, NY 10011; phone: 212/645-0770).

Another organization you may want to consider is the American Society for Training and Development. Maybe someday you will want to expand your memberships to the larger groups affiliated with your company.

If you need further direction about professional associations, your local library will have the reference book *Encyclopedia of Associations*, published by Gale Research Company. It categorizes all the associations in the United States according to what they do.

Rise Above the Angst

There is a popular feminist attitude, a kind of *martyrdom* that some women assume. Not only is this attitude bad for your professional image, it's bad for *you*. Every person has freedom and is responsible for his or her actions and attitudes. We are all just *people*, trying hard to be happy and successful. If you feel sometimes like the world is out to get you or that your company is unfair to you, step out of the situation for a moment and ask yourself, "How important is this—really—compared to my peace of mind?"

Billy makes tons of money selling advertising specialties. Most salespeople will tell you how much pressure there is in a sales job and how competitive it is. But not Billy. Her business keeps getting better and better, and she's one of the calmest and most easygoing people I know. How does she do it? Her motto is this: "I don't take anything too seriously."

Incidentally, if the world does seem to be out to get you and your company is being unfair, an attitude of "I'm so oppressed" will get you nowhere. In fact, your salvation lies in a *positive* attitude. If your work situation is unbearable and for one reason or another you are stuck with it for a while, follow this advice. You'll be surprised at how much better things get.

Or, if there's someone in your life you can't get along with (and you need to), just *love* that person to death. Go out of your way to be thoughtful and considerate. Doing so will accomplish two important things. First, that person will lose his or her negative power over you. Second, your relationship will be stronger.

Office Romances

As Betty Lehan Harragan, author of *Games Mother Never Taught You*, has recognized, sex is a business problem.[5] As recently as November 1988, *Working Woman* reported that prevailing wisdom still advises against office romance. But in 1986, 40 percent of the women polled by the magazine reported having an affair at the office—a number that could be even higher now.[6] So, although most sources agree that, ideally, office romance shouldn't even exist, they also acknowledge that in reality it does.

For those of you who are (or will be) involved in an office romance, the article gives this advice for maintaining a professional image:

1. Set up periodic emotional checkpoints to evaluate your feelings and reactions.

2. Don't feel that you must continue the relationship simply because you have begun.

3. Be discreet. Neither one of you should be a source of gossip or rumor.

4. Don't leave cute messages or notes—or touch each other inappropriately in the office. This makes others feel excluded.

5. Keep job performance high. Corporate response will be strongly influenced by whether your work is affected.

6. Don't bring personal matters into the office—or vice versa. If there's a status differential, respect the boundaries.

7. Don't speak for each other at work or indicate that you have special "inside" knowledge. Such insider knowledge makes others feel threatened.[7]

Think of Men as People

Learn how to talk to men. Actually, this tip is a little misleading. It should be "learn how to talk to people." As far as your professional life goes, men are just people. They are not parents, mates, saviors, or fools. They are coworkers. Sometimes it's hard to remember this because so many of us were raised with the notion that men and women have different and well-defined roles in society. Certainly, the traditional view still holds men to be the primary breadwinners and women to be their support systems. That "reality," however, simply no longer applies.

Breaking the Glass Ceiling, a book published in 1987, states that 33 percent of America's corporate middle management is female. The Internal Revenue Service reports that women own 2.8 million companies in the United States, and according to another report, 3.5 million women are self-employed. And these figures don't account for the millions of women working in positions below middle management![8]

Stereotypes tell us that men like to talk about things and events, while women like to talk about people and feelings. Maybe that's a good thing to remember in the beginning of a relationship. For example, when you make a sales call on Mr. Williams, director of product design for the Tank Division of the International Conflict Corporation, don't open your conversation with a story about what your 18-month-old did with her creamed spinach the night before.

Even better advice is to treat people as *individuals*. Find out and remember the interests of the people you have relationships with. You will find that there are both men and women who like to talk about how great the San Francisco 49ers are and that there are both men and women who will talk for hours about their children. What if Mr. Williams, in the previous example, has pictures of his 18-month-old twin grandchildren all over his office? Perhaps your creamed spinach story would add a personal touch he'd welcome.

Treat people like people. And don't forget: Professionally, *we* are just people too. We are not mothers, wives, or dates. As women, we need to stick together and support each other as coworkers, but we also need to stick together and support each other as people.

We need to let go of our rigid stereotypes about male versus female behaviors if we hope to become more successful in our careers. Don't be afraid to be assertive! But don't feel you have to give up your compassion either. Professional men and women in the 1990s will need *both* those traits as well as many others previously considered the domain of only one sex. A little androgyny never hurt anyone. Androgyny, as it pertains to your professional image, is just a fancy way of saying that we are all just people.

You are a whole person, and as a whole person, you can invest yourself in your future. The payback will come in your happiness, your fulfillment, and your success.

Endnotes

1. Leah Rosch, "The Professional Image Report: What Matters, What Doesn't," *Working Woman*, 13(10) (October 1988): 109.

2. Melody Sharp Quarnstrom, *Getting On Top* (Los Angeles: Price Stern Sloan, 1988), 61.

3. Janet Dight, *Breaking the Secretary Barrier* (New York: McGraw-Hill, 1988), 127-129.

4. Mary Bridgett Carroll, *Overworked and Underpaid* (New York: Fawcett Columbine, 1983), 200.

5. Betty Lehan Harragan, *Games Mother Never Taught You* (New York: Warner, 1978).

6. Harriet B. Braiker, "The Etiquette of Office Romance," *Working Woman* 13 (November 1988): 148.

7. Ibid., 153.

8. Ann M. Morrison, Randall P. White, Ellen Van Velsor, and the Center for Creative Leadership, *Breaking the Glass Ceiling* (Reading, MA: Addison Wesley, 1987), 5.

3

MANAGEMENT SAVVY

Leadership: The art of getting someone else to do something you want done because he (or she) wants to do it.
— Dwight D. Eisenhower

Genius is the talent for seeing things straight. It is seeing things in a straight line without any bend or aberration of sight, seeing them as they are, without any warping of vision.
— Maude Adams

The very essence of leadership is (that) you have to have a vision. It's got to be a vision you articulate clearly and forcefully on every occasion. You can't blow an uncertain trumpet.
— Fr. Theodore Hesburgh,
(former president, Notre Dame University)

If you are a woman recently promoted (or hoping to be promoted) to a management position, this chapter is for you. The transition can be tough. If you are promoted to supervise people who used to be your peers, you may feel guilty treating them as support workers. Or you may have worked hard to get to this new position, only to find that it requires a whole new set of skills you hadn't even considered. Whatever your situation, the success tips in this chapter will help you change your mind-set from that of a subordinate to one of a manager.

Even if you haven't been promoted yet, it is still a good idea to try these new behaviors. You will be seen more readily as management material, and your new attitude will probably get you the attention you need sooner.

Think Like a Manager

William Yeomans, author of *1000 Things You Never Learned in Business School*, maintains that anyone who wants to get ahead should have a realistic view of how things are and a long-range vision of how they should be.[1] Even if you're not a manager yet, think as if you were; you'll be more prepared for the position when it comes.

Develop your ability to see reality clearly. Then think about the way things *should* be. What are the differences? What changes need to be made? Who needs to make them? Try to think of an action plan that would get your department or your organization where it should be. But remember not to lose your realistic view of the present. There's no use being angry or frustrated every day until you finally get to your Utopia—keep your progress (or lack of it) in perspective.

Have a Career Goal

Set a career goal and make sure it's realistic. Remember, you're climbing the *ladder* of success and you must climb some of the lower rungs before you can get a view from the top. Still, you should always keep your eye on the job two or three tiers up from you. What do you need to do to get there? Are there educational requirements? Must you spend a certain amount of time with the organization first? Do your best to find out what the qualifications are and plan how you can meet them.

Set Priorities

Focus on your priorities, and delegate jobs or shift responsibilities for tasks not rightfully yours. Concentrate on your basic duties or other more *visible* things you could be doing to advance your career. If you find yourself in over your head, *say so.*

Use All Your Strength

Zig Ziglar, in his fabulous book *Top Performance*, tells a story
of a little boy trying and trying—in vain—to move a heavy log
in order to clear a path to his favorite hideout. His dad finally
asked him why he wasn't using all his strength. The boy
explained that he was straining as hard as he could. The father
quietly disagreed, telling his son that if he was using all his
strength, he would've asked him to help.

According to Ziglar, successful managers recognize, develop,
and use the physical, mental, and spiritual talents of those they
supervise. These managers "learn what makes people tick, and
they transfer their own excitement and enthusiasm to those who
follow their leadership."[2]

Accept Personal Responsibility

Accepting personal responsibility is actually another way of
saying "Don't blame—fix the cause." But it also means that if
there is something that needs to be fixed and it's in your power
to fix it, you really must.

Be a role model for your people. Accept personal responsibility
for your mistakes and your poor decisions. Show your
employees and coworkers that you are willing to take action to
make things better. If you show your people how a job is
supposed to be done and that you are not interested in punishing
them when things go wrong, you will be well on your way to
establishing a truly creative and productive working group.

Ken Follett's book *On Wings of Eagles* portrays one man's
willingness to accept personal responsibility. The man Follett
wrote about is Ross Perot, founder of Electronic Data Systems
(EDS). In December 1978, amid turbulent domestic upheavals
and growing anti-American sentiment in Iran, two top EDS
executives were captured by Iranians and imprisoned. Mr. Perot
and his key executives in the United States mapped out a plan to

rescue the two men. (The group didn't have much faith that the U.S. government would be able to help, given the delicate political situation.) Perot's plan included staging a riot in Iran, breaking into the prison, and freeing the two executives. Extreme measures, to say the least. But Perot and his men carried out their plan successfully, freeing the two employees from a nearly hopeless situation.[3]

In 1985 Perot sold EDS to General Motors, making him one of the richest people in the world. One of the reasons he became so successful was his willingness to take personal responsibility.

Find Good in Others

If you look for the good in your coworkers, they will appreciate it and you will appreciate their renewed enthusiasm. Give sincere compliments to the people you manage. By focusing on their good qualities and their victories, you will increase those good qualities and victories. Have you ever habitually berated someone? That person just seems to get worse before your eyes, right?

Focusing on the positive is a tool that becomes even more necessary as you rise up the corporate ladder. As a manager of people, it should be your primary goal. Try this experiment:

For just one day, don't say anything negative. If you're tempted, just stay silent or find something good to comment on. Make a point of giving sincere compliments to the people you manage, especially to the ones who have annoyed you recently. You will see results.

Two important principles are involved here. First, when you seek to appreciate the good in others, their good points magnify. Second, when you program yourself to dwell on what is working in your department or in your people, you find more things that *are* working.

This isn't to say that when someone makes a mistake, you shouldn't make sure she or he knows how to avoid that same mistake in the future. But once you've fixed it, forget it. Focus on the positive.

Learn to Listen

The next time one of your employees comes into your office to talk to you, clear your mind. Don't think about what you'll say or about your history of troubles with the person. Just open your mind and listen. It will put you in a much better position to respond. (If this tip sounds like something that could help you, look into a listening skills tape or book.)

Give Specific Feedback

Employees appreciate feedback on their work. Be sure to make *specific* comments. Specific feedback will keep your employees growing in the directions that will help them most. They will have a concrete idea of the areas in which they are succeeding as well as of the areas in which they need to improve. And remember, when your feedback is negative, always direct it toward the action, not the person.

Compare the following examples of positive and negative feedback:

Positive

Example 1: "Jane, you did a great job on this project. I'm especially impressed with the way you pulled all the pieces together at the end—and in so little time! Thanks for your hard work."

Example 2: "Jane, you're a great secretary!"

Negative

Example 1: "Jane, thanks for your hard work on this project. It took longer than I was hoping, though. Is there something we need to change in our time planning for projects like these?"

Example 2: "Jane, you never do ANYTHING right."

See how the first examples are better in each case? The comments are nonpersonal, addressing the action or the task, not the employee. Further, the feedback is specific. In the positive example, Jane is commended for her organizational skills and timeliness. In the negative example, the time frame of the project is questioned and the supervisor provides Jane with an opportunity to offer suggestions for improving the schedule.

Learn to Say "No"

Although cooperation should be your watchword, there are limits. As a manager, it's your obligation to protect the interests of your organization. And as an employee, it's your duty to put your foot down—gracefully—when your boss or coworkers go too far.

If saying no is a problem for you, join the club. But while you're waiting for your membership card, think seriously about enrolling in some assertiveness training. At the very least, read a book on the subject. In the meantime, consider using the following techniques.

Consider the Consequences Technique

Your boss has just asked you to move the deadline for your month-end financial report up a week. Use simple logic. In order for you to finish your month-end financial report by the end of the week, you will have to cancel your audit trip to the Denver office. And if you cancel the Denver trip, the company could lose more than $5,000 in product returns. Leave the choice for your boss to make.

The "I'd Love to But I Can't" Technique

This approach requires developing a fairly inflexible reason for why you can't do what is being requested or ordered and then suggesting helpful alternatives (none of which include your giving in). This is an excellent technique to use when someone has clearly gone too far.

For example, you are the manager of customer service. Hugh Aldrich, the payroll manager, needs a report typed by the next morning for the company's president. It contains a lot of confidential information he doesn't want his secretary to see, so he comes to you—at 4:55—and asks you to type it for him.

You say: "Oh, I'm sorry, Hugh, I really can't. My brother is flying in from Los Angeles tonight, and I have to pick him up at the airport at 6:00. Maybe you should ask the president if he'd have his secretary type it for you in the morning. She handles all his confidential material regularly, and I know he trusts her."

Notice that this technique involves Hugh in the consequences of his action—waiting until the last minute to ask you to do this favor for him—instead of placing the burden on you.

Make Tantrums Count

Know when to throw a fit. Or rather, know when to throw a fit effectively.

In their book *Strategies for Women at Work*, Janice LaRouche and Regina Ryan use Dorothea as an example. Her request for funds to hire a consulting company to test market the new product she had been working on for ten months was shelved in a meeting by the vice president of marketing on the basis that the whole company was cutting expenses. Dorothea tried to be reasonable yet assertive in arguing her case (which usually worked for her). But she got nowhere. She had great faith in her idea, and it was important to her that it be given a fair chance.

Finally, she stood up, slammed down her papers and said: "What's the matter with you people? It's the best product idea we've had in 16 years. This is a disaster."[4] And she stormed out without a backward glance. A couple of hours later, that vice president came to her office to talk about the project again and conceded quickly to her wishes.

Now, according to LaRouche and Ryan, here's the important part:

> As often happens when someone throws a fit, he [the vice president] had gotten less sure of himself. People see the firmness of your belief, and thus their own view is shaken. Moreover, the passion of your reaction will make them concerned about the possible disruption of a good working relationship. Rather than worry about your anger, they will try to appease you.[5]

And here's their disclaimer:

> Throwing a fit can be a very powerful move, but to be effective, tantrums should be few and far between. And don't attempt to throw a fit if your company is one of those uptight outfits that doesn't permit disruptions of its even-tempered atmosphere.[6]

Use your own intuitive judgment to decide whether throwing a fit is an option for you. Weigh the situation carefully: Are you respected enough by your company that expressing your feelings in this way will help you? (Or maybe you have a better job lined up already, and you won last week's lottery to boot.)

Whatever you do, don't take this advice as license to blow up whenever you're frustrated and want your own way. List all the times you *don't* blow up. That way if you're accused of being hotheaded, you can ask why, if you're so hotheaded, you didn't blow up about . . . (fill in just one item from your list). It will help *you* to read your whole list to yourself to remind you of how reasonable you are. But telling your accuser about all the times you managed to check your anger would make his or her accusation pretty much true, wouldn't it?

Acquire Spending Savvy

Understand money from management's perspective. Don't be surprised to hear "no," and don't take it personally. Many times money decisions are made to keep from setting a precedent—not to slap your hands.

Learn as much as you're permitted about the company's finances. This is not an area for snooping, though. Bosses like employees to show interest in the company, but most of them get a little nervous when you get too interested in the financial picture. Remember, the goal of this book is to improve your chances for career success—not to make the managers of your organization suspicious of your intentions.

Become an Intrapreneur

Rosabeth Moss Kanter defines an intrapreneur as a corporate entrepreneur—not someone who starts a new business, but someone who improves an existing business. Of course, an employee who improves the company's business tends to advance in the company.

Intrapreneurs generally operate in three stages. First, they formulate and sell a vision. Next, they find the power to advance their ideas. And, finally, they work to maintain the momentum. Kanter lists the six primary skills all intrapreneurs seem to share.

1. *Kaleidoscope thinking.* This involves twisting your perspective, or focusing on existing information from another angle, and then analyzing the new patterns and shapes you see.

2. *Communicating a vision.* Somebody must be willing to stand behind the new idea and keep pushing, because when change

is involved, things tend to get difficult. How many good ideas have been abandoned because there was no one communicating belief when things got tough? Notice that Martin Luther King Jr. didn't say, "I have a few *ideas*; maybe if we set up a committee, something will happen." He said, "I have a *dream*."

3. *Persistence, persistence, persistence.* Intrapreneurs stay with the project long enough to make it work. To some extent, every project looks like a failure about halfway through. And nay sayers are always more likely to surface at that time because that's when new ways start threatening the status quo. Successful intrapreneurs don't give up.

4. *Building a coalition.* Selling your ideas means building a group of supporters. Without support, you and your ideas are powerless.

5. *Working in teams.* Successful intrapreneurs have the ability to build a working team to carry out the idea. Full involvement is essential when change is being introduced; very few ideas of any significance are put into motion by a solitary individual.

6. *Sharing of credit.* People who lead changes share credit and make everyone a hero. This helps to make change an opportunity rather than a threat.

Recognize and Exploit Lucky Breaks

Understand that lucky breaks don't just happen. How many times have you heard an associate's success belittled with a comment like, "Well, she was in the right place at the right time." Maybe so—but you can be sure she *put* herself into that right place. Max Gunther, author of *The Luck Factor,* says, "If you want to change your luck, change your attitude."[7] According to Gunther, here are ten characteristics (that anyone can learn to have) that lucky people seem to share:

1. They are extroverts.

2. They have magnetic personalities.

3. They're in touch with their feelings.

4. They know the difference between a hunch and a hope.

5. They do their homework.

6. They recognize an opportunity when it comes along.

7. They are prepared to take risks.

8. They are skeptics—they always have a fallback solution worked out in advance.

9. They know when to quit—while they're still ahead. They stick with their decisions only as long as the situation continues to produce the desired results.

10. They can admit their mistakes.

Become More Like Mary Kay Ash ————————————

Mary Kay Ash is the founder of Mary Kay Cosmetics and one of the most successful businesswomen of our day. In 1983, on the twentieth anniversary of her company (it grossed over $300 million that year), Mary Kay published a book titled *Mary Kay on People Management* describing her theory of Golden Rule Management.[8]

Golden Rule Management, as its name implies, boils down to treating staff, customers, suppliers, and everyone else in the same manner you'd like for them to treat you. Specifically, her book teaches you to:

1. Recognize the value of people.

2. Praise your people to success.

3. Tear down the ivory tower and be accessible to everyone.

4. Be a risk-taker.

5. Be sales oriented.

6. Be a problem solver.

7. Create a stress-free workplace.

8. Develop and promote people from within.

9. Keep business in its proper place.

If you want to learn how to be a better manager, reading Mary Kay's book is a must. Written by a very successful businesswoman from her own experience, it's one of the most enjoyable books on management skills available.

Endnotes

1. William Yeomans, *1000 Things You Never Learned in Business School* (New York: McGraw-Hill, 1985).

2. Zig Ziglar, *Top Performance* (Old Tappan, NJ: Fleming H. Revell, 1986), 11.

3. Ken Follett, *On Wings of Eagles* (New York: William Morrow, 1983).

4. Janice LaRouche and Regina Ryan, *Strategies for Women at Work* (New York: Avon, 1984), 333.

5. Ibid.

6. Ibid.

7. Max Gunther, *The Luck Factor* (New York: Macmillan, 1977).

8. Mary Kay Ash, *Mary Kay on People Management* (New York: Warner, 1984), xv.

PERSONAL PUBLIC RELATIONS

Many competent managers fail to rise within their organizations because
they overlook a vital career consideration—
the need to "promote themselves."
— James L. Hayes, former president
American Management Association

You don't have to like or admire your boss, nor do you have to hate him.
You do have to manage him, however, so that he becomes your resource for
achievement, accomplishment, and personal success.
— Peter Drucker

Self-promotion is just another name for marketing yourself. Just as press agents make sure that the media pick up stories about their clients, you must now become your *own* press agent to make sure that news of your promotability gets around.

This chapter teaches you the basics of marketing yourself. You'll find three main avenues for this activity: general self-promotion, boss relations, and networking. Learning to use all three will benefit you as much as contacts in television, radio, and print benefit a press agent.

Find a Project You Can Call Your Own

Volunteer for a project and work hard to do a good job on it. By having tangible proof of your own good work, you will gain visibility. People will be able to look at it when it's done and say, "Didn't Jennifer do a great job on that?"

Announce Accomplishments

Drop hints about how much you've accomplished to the people
in charge. Again, there's nothing wrong with a little honest
advertising: "Boy, we've managed to contact sixty prospective
clients today and send them brochures!" Let people know how
well you and your department are doing. Don't be heavy-
handed, though. And certainly don't whine: "Mr. Rosen, we've
already contacted sixty prospective clients today and sent them
brochures." Be positive and enthusiastic, and the right people
will notice.

Write, Write, Write

Does writing scare you? Look around at the people in your
organization who have the positions you'd like to have someday.
Notice what they have in common: the memo.

In most organizations, memo writing is a rite of passage
between a support position and management. As you move up
the corporate ladder, your business writing skills become more
and more important. Managers use memos to talk to each other
and to those they manage.

If you are not confident of your writing skills, do something now
to improve them. Take a class or a seminar in business writing.
While you're there, buy a good reference book on the subject. If
you have trouble with grammar or spelling, find a self-study
guide to help you.

Keep a file of well-written memos, reports, and letters. Label
the file "Prototypes." Don't be concerned with who wrote the
memo, only with how *well* it is written. Is it direct? Easy to
understand? Did its author make his or her point in as few
words as possible? Are the words and sentences easy to
understand? Is it written in a conversational style? Is the format
easy to follow? Study the memos to learn what makes them
good and to familiarize yourself with the standards of your
organization. And then start writing.

If you are still not convinced that memos are necessary, remember this important fact: Memos (and copies of them) can go many places that you normally cannot.

Attend Trade Conventions

Trade conventions are a great place to learn a lot more about your business in a short amount of time. Tell your boss you'd like to attend, and prepare some good reasons why it would benefit the company if you did. Does your company have an exhibit at the convention? Then say you'd love to work at the booth. Or explain that you are very interested in becoming more active in the professional association (remember — you joined it back in the first chapter) and how doing so could benefit the company.

If going to a national convention is too much to expect, see if there's a local meeting or a regional conference you could attend. These, too, are great occasions for networking.

If you do attend a convention, sample a little of everything. Spend some time in workshops and educational sessions, some time on the exhibit hall floor, and some in the lounges. Talk with other attendees. Network—make it your goal to take home at least ten names and phone numbers—and then keep in touch with those people. This is how networks and support groups are built.

When you return from any of these sessions, you should prepare a full report of your trip for the manager who okayed your attendance. While you're at it, include a handwritten thank you note.

Learn to Present Your Ideas

You don't need to be a professional speaker to get ahead in your career, but you do need to be able to communicate your ideas—

and sometimes to people who intimidate you. Learn how to speak in front of anyone. There are plenty of good books on this topic, but probably the best education you'll ever get is more personal. Do you have a friend with a video camera? Ask your friend to tape you giving a presentation.

When Sheila had the opportunity to give a presentation to the vice president in charge of new developments at her company, she knew that she had a lot of work ahead of her. Although she had taken a speech class in college, it had been a long time since she had spoken formally. So she asked her friend, Ellen, to videotape her presentation.

Sheila was amazed at how much she learned. The flaws in her presentation style were immediately apparent. And they were things she could change without too much effort. She could get a new haircut so she wouldn't keep pushing her bangs out of her eyes. She could stop tilting her head to the right when she wanted the audience to believe her. She could look less stern when she was trying to be sincere.

Today, Sheila is the manager of her own department—a position that stems from the presentation she gave. She vows that being taped was one of the most valuable experiences of her career.

Keep an Achievement File

Make it a priority to keep a current file of positive reviews, thank you letters from satisfied clients, copies of invoices for important sales, and any other tokens of personal business victories. Such items serve as ammunition when you approach your boss about a raise or promotion, certainly. But they are also good when you need a quick pick-me-up to keep motivated on a less-than-great day. Keep the file in your desk, someplace where you'll notice it often.

Cultivate Allies

Cultivate allies from day one. All the materials I've ever seen on career success agree about this: Networking is vital to getting ahead. Make contacts from your very first day.

The best way to cultivate an ally is to be one. Show people from day one that you're interested in their success and that you won't gossip about their mistakes. Your integrity is the first ingredient that will attract others to you.

Once you are more familiar with the politics of your organization, you may want to select your allies more carefully. But—particularly at the beginning—don't overlook your peers. Today's coworker could be tomorrow's manager. Put the same energy into those relationships as you do into your relationship with your mentor.

Join an Employee Club or Team

Are you a good softball player? Or do you like to exercise? Most large organizations have clubs, teams, and programs open to any employee. They are a great way to get to know the people you work with better—and to let them get to know you. To really become familiar with someone, it's helpful to see him or her in more than one role (not just as director of marketing). Many times you will be able to meet and get to know people from different departments, or managers further up the corporate ladder, that you normally wouldn't have access to.

Trade Information Judiciously

Trade information with good sources only. There is no reason to exchange information with complainers or unreliable people. When you receive information, always consider the source. Incidentally, the most valuable information you can get from your coworkers is how to deal with the various personalities in your office. Make sure to find out who can get things done.

Make Your Boss Feel Important

Making your boss feel important at all times is a more specific way of stating Dale Carnegie's tenet: "If you make people feel important, they will like you." For example, never leave your boss waiting in the doorway of your office while you finish a phone call with your husband about where to meet after work. Occasionally, it may be OK to leave your boss in the doorway while you're finishing up a business call—with an important client of the company, for example, or with your distributor who's calling from Germany. But, as a general rule, make sure that you put your boss first while you're at work.

Ask your boss what he or she thinks about a current business dilemma. Or ask to hear again the story about how she or he was called on to give an impromptu speech for the board of directors last year and ended up with new computers for everyone in the department.

Use the golden rule discussed in Chapter 3. Treat your boss with the respect and concern you expect to be treated with. And remember that we're all just people—even your boss.

Listen to Your Boss

Pay attention to what your boss means, not just to what she or he says. Be a good listener. We discussed this earlier, in relation to the people you manage, but it applies to your boss as well. Be such a good listener that you understand even the *unspoken* message he or she generates.

For example, your boss stops at your office for an update on your progress with The Big Project. While there, she or he reaches over and straightens the papers you have been tossing in your "in" box all morning. The spoken message? "I'm interested in hearing about your progress." The unspoken one? "I like things to be neat." The moral? Keep your boss informed about your progress *and* keep your desk neat.

Don't Gossip

Don't gossip, especially about your boss. Not ever, no matter what.

Take Charge

Your boss says, "I've got to get these figures together for the Board by Monday, and I just don't know when I'm going to have the time." Speak up! Say, "If you can think of someone else to meet with John about the new spreadsheet program this afternoon, I'll be happy to help."

Don't be so overcome by your everyday routine and your fixed responsibilities that you miss the opportunity to do something new—and visible.

Help Your Boss Look Good

Someone very smart once said that anyone can make career progress in any organization, even in a huge, highly structured one. Take positive action and make sure your contributions are known and recognized by your superiors. Know your boss (and how she or he operates), and work at your very best level to help her or him. In this day and age, you cannot make career progress by killing off your superiors in the hope of occupying their chairs. It is only in a *progressive* situation that you can grow. By pushing someone who is ahead of you along, you can fill the seat when that person is promoted.

For the Advanced Student Only:
Getting Your Boss to Change

In their book on solving the problem of problem bosses, Drs. Mardell Grothe and Peter Wylie say that in some cases, you can change your boss through a one-on-one talk. They give instructions for this talk, from setting the appointment and preparing your material to having the discussion and responding to your boss's resistance. The following paragraphs present their advice in a nutshell.[1]

Prepare for the meeting. Ask yourself two questions: What does my boss do that helps make my job satisfying and fulfilling? What could my boss do to make my job less frustrating and more satisfying? Write out the answers to these questions and list examples for each point. Be specific.

Make an appointment. Do this in person, when your boss is alone and not busy—but not if you're angry. Get your boss's reaction to the idea of a meeting to discuss how the two of you can improve your working relationship. Then explain that you will be thinking of specific changes you'd like to see in your job and in how you're managed. Suggest that your boss do a similar performance analysis for you. Pick a meeting place that's comfortable and free of distractions. On your way out, make a positive comment like: "I'm looking forward to this meeting. I think we'll both get a lot out of it."

Have the meeting. Make your boss comfortable by talking casually to start. Then state the purpose of the meeting: "I think we're here to talk about and agree on some ways the two of us can improve our working relationship. I see us as working reasonably well together already, but there's always room for improvement. This meeting can start that improvement."

Then come right out and ask, "What can I do to make your job more satisfying and less frustrating?" Then listen. Don't argue or defend. Listen to everything—the words, the body language, the attitude. If you want your boss to change, first you have to be willing to change. If you want your boss to listen to you, your best bet is to listen to your boss. Start by encouraging your boss to give you feedback. When she or he finishes, summarize what was said. Make sure that you leave nothing out and that you understand correctly.

Now it's your turn. Ease into the exchange by first discussing the positive points on your list, the things your boss does that make you feel good about your job. Give concrete examples. Then move into the real reason you wanted this meeting—the things you'd like changed. When giving feedback, always be prepared to stop talking and start listening. If your boss starts showing signs of wanting to say something, let her or him speak. Then read back what was said. This is the best way to keep your boss receptive. Stay away from emotionally loaded expressions.

When you have both finished talking, work up a performance agreement (make sure there's something in it for both of you) and schedule a follow-up meeting.

Handling the Boss's Anger

Most likely, you are afraid to make your boss angry. And generally that is a healthy fear. But bosses are human—to expect them never to get angry with you is unreasonable.

Some people think that the best way to handle a boss's anger is to defend yourself—to deny the accusation, explain why the offending act was committed, or become indignant in return.

But there is a better way.

When someone is venting anger at you, that person is not at that moment open to reason, defense, rationalization, or returned anger. The best thing to do is just let him or her go. Don't react. Just nod occasionally and say "uh huh" if it is appropriate. Pretend that you are in group therapy and that you must give this person the respect of an uninterrupted turn.

This technique will save you the time it takes to argue with someone who is not rational. One angry tirade is hard enough for a relationship to recover from; dueling tirades are twice as bad. Save your reputation and your sanity: detach.

Assess Your Company

Finally, evaluate the reality of your present situation. Does your company or organization have potential? Do you come into contact with other well-run companies and professionals? If you sought an interview with one of your organization's competitors, would it be interested in you just because of the company you work for right now?

If your company isn't gaining momentum, or at least holding its own, look out. You may be able to advance to the position of president in a failing organization, but would doing so really help you in the long run? Certainly, this is not to suggest that a company experiencing a setback should be abandoned. But check to see whether a pattern is developing. Is management willing to meet the demands of the marketplace? Is the company run by people unwilling to change with the times? If you have doubts about where your organization is headed, it's best to get out *before* the last hurrah. And if you have doubts about your doubts, take a look at Tom Peters' book *Thriving on Chaos*.[2] Measure your company against his prescriptions, but not so much to see if it's there today. Instead, ask yourself whether the leadership of your company would *ever* buy into any of what Peters has to say.

Next ask yourself: Does my particular job have career potential? Am I learning the "how to" of a particular field? Is my job interesting? Does it have potential beyond the scope of my present duties?

If you've asked yourself all these questions and most of the answers are "yes," you're in luck. Keep practicing the other suggestions in this book and expect to be promoted—soon.

But if your answers are "no" and you are committed to getting ahead in your career, there is probably only one solution: Change companies. You may even want to change your career.

Find a company and a position with *potential*. Even an interim position that teaches you new skills and moves you closer to your career goal is a better alternative than an uninspiring dead-end job that offers security. While you're at it, think about breaking away from traditionally female and overcrowded job fields and into more promising, male-dominated areas of business, science, and technology.

To get ahead, the bottom line is that you must be willing to put yourself on the line. To become a leader, you must act. People who are management material have the ability and the willingness to take risks, but they also exercise discipline. If you're already an expert at your present job, you probably belong in a better one.

Endnotes

1. Mardell Grothe and Peter Wylie, *Problem Bosses: Who They Are and How to Deal with Them* (New York: Facts on File, 1987), 150-189.

2. Tom Peters, *Thriving on Chaos: Handbook for a Management Revolution* (New York: Knopf, 1987).

5

PERSONAL POWER

There were many ways of breaking a heart. Stories were full of hearts broken by love, but what really broke a heart was taking away its dream—whatever that dream might be.
— Pearl S. Buck

Power is strength and the ability to see yourself through your own eyes and not through the eyes of another. It is being able to place a circle of power at your own feet and not take power from someone else's circle.
— Agnes Whistling Elk

Don't compromise yourself—you're all you've got.
— Janis Joplin

Given the importance of this subject, perhaps this chapter should have come first. You can possess all the titles, all the education and all the admirers in the world, but if you do not know and love yourself, you will still feel empty during those strange, lonely moments so many of us experience.

Personal power comes from many things, but most writers agree that its origin is in our hearts and in our souls. Knowledge alone does not bring happiness. Neither does money, prestige, expensive cars, or yachts.

As a matter of fact, some people like Napoleon Hill, author of *Think and Grow Rich*, go so far as to say that personal power generally comes *before* we achieve success or acquire material wealth—that the world's most successful people learned how to believe in *themselves* before achieving their fantastic successes.[1]

Of all the advice in this book, perhaps the most important (and the hardest to follow) is to *believe in yourself*. The most valuable commodity you have in your climb to the top is you—*the real you*. If you don't have a good concept of who that is, or if you find it hard to look at yourself in the mirror and say, "(Fill in name), you are a wonderful and capable woman, beautiful in heart and soul," take this chapter very seriously. Use the techniques it offers as a starting point, and find other help elsewhere.

Power begins with your self-image. And the journey to a positive self-image is the most worthwhile trip you'll ever take. Good luck in your travels.

Know Thyself

Know thyself. Socrates said it first, and you've heard it many times since. Do what you can to know and love yourself. Obviously this small handbook can't scratch the surface of all the self-help material available today. But check the Bibliography for a starting place, or pick up a book or a set of tapes that appeals to you and get started. How *much* you accomplish is not as important as how *regularly* you try. Make getting to know more about yourself a lifelong hobby.

To Thine Own Self Be True

Maintain your integrity—even when those around you don't. No matter how angry you are or how cheated you feel, accept the fact that any slip of your integrity could destroy two very important things: all the work you've done to look good and, more important, your self-respect.

There is no excuse or reason to compromise your principles. But use your judgment. Many things are just not important enough to fuss about. Did you ever work with someone who threatened to go to the boss, or called a lawyer, or just plain quit over some matter you considered trivial—like having his or her lunch hour switched to another time?

Before you lose your temper, ask yourself this question: Is the thing I am so upset about really important to me, right down to my soul? Or am I hurt and threatened and not in a position to think clearly right now?

Inspire Yourself

Find an interest and involve yourself in it passionately. You are a powerful woman; show the world you are a mover by allowing yourself to be moved by something. Do not, however, cross the line from passion to obsession. Your enthusiasm for life is one of the best tools you have for getting ahead.

Push Yourself

Reach. Do things you don't like to do, just for practice. As a matter of fact, make doing something you don't want to do a special item on your agenda each day. And why not also add this: Do one anonymous good deed each day. Do something nice for someone else—and don't get caught.

Neither of these tasks has to be very large or time consuming. You could add paper to the copier when it's running low. You could casually mention to Jan's boss how Jan has so willingly taken on some of your extra work in the past week. Don't mention this to Jan, of course.

If you push yourself to accomplish these two goals every day for two weeks, your self-assurance and personal power will grow by leaps and bounds. Give it a try.

Be an Optimist

Optimists have the power to master change—and to empower others to triumph over challenges. The secret of being an optimist? Believing that *you*—not outside forces—control your future. *Working Woman* magazine published these ten ways to develop an optimist's eye:

1. Consciously set goals.

2. Acquire a sense of control by doing your homework.

3. Anticipate success.

4. Imagine the worst-case scenario and have a plan of action ready for it. (This is your psychological safety net.)

5. Be good to yourself.

6. Surround yourself with successful, positive people.

7. Don't fight negative thoughts; accept them and move on to your next task. (Fighting them only makes them come back later.)

8. Keep your body tuned.

9. Look good to feel good.

10. Don't live at the office.[2]

Do Not Fear Failure

Get rid of your fear of failure. Of course, you are going to make some mistakes; you're supposed to. It's one of the best ways you have of learning. And you can't win all the time either; sometimes you will fail. It doesn't matter so much what happens *to* you. What matters is *how you handle the peaks and valleys of your life.*

It's been said that there's nothing wrong with making a mistake, only with compounding that mistake by defending it. Admit to yours quickly and move on. You'll be stronger for it, and you'll inspire confidence in others that you are in control.

Take Care of Your Body

Obviously whole books could be written—and have been—on the subject of caring for yourself physically. If you're not feeling totally well, consider whether one of these common trouble spots for working women is the source of your problem:

1. Are you eating regularly? Getting enough fruit, vegetables, protein, whole grains, and milk? (Remember the four food groups from elementary school?)

2. Do you think that one of those four food groups is the "chocolate and potato chip" group? Are you eating too much junk food? ("How much is too much?" you ask. Are you eating junk food instead of a meal?)

3. Do you get any exercise? Do you take a twenty-minute walk before work? Do you attend exercise classes a couple evenings a week? You don't need hours of exercise per day. In fact, if you don't exercise now, the worst thing you could do is exercise for two hours tonight after you read this. Start slowly. It's more important to form the habit of exercising regularly than to exercise strenuously. Set aside ten minutes at the most convenient time for you each day and do something physical. Do it every day for a month, and don't push yourself to spend more than those ten minutes at it. By the end of the month, you'll probably have the habit, and it will be less of an effort to increase your time, if you want to.

4. Do you get six to seven hours of sleep every night? If you find yourself too wound up to sleep, try getting those ten minutes of exercise right before bed. Or spend a little time outside, or take a warm bubble bath by candlelight, or drink a cup of herbal tea.

5. Do you smoke cigarettes? Sorry, but all the facts are in; *none* of them are good. Do yourself a favor: Put quitting on the top of your "to do" list.

6. Do you use "recreational" drugs? Do you drink too much? If you think either of these things is a problem for you, get help. Many companies have employee assistance programs for alcoholics and addicts. There are thousands of additional treatment centers nationwide. Alcoholics Anonymous (AA) is as close as your telephone. (Look in your yellow pages under Alcoholism.) As Lou Reed says in his public service announcement on MTV: "I used to do drugs. Now I don't." The days when it was cool to be a druggie are over. Enough said.

Take Care of Your Mental Health

AA has a slogan that you may have seen on bumper stickers: *Easy Does It.* H.A.L.T. Don't get too hungry, too angry, too lonely, or too tired. Those things all lead to distorted thinking.

Take a break when you need one. Spend some time outside every day and become involved in something besides your work. You are your most important commodity. Make sure you treat yourself at least as well as you would your best friend.

Try Affirmations

Affirmations are positive statements you make aloud, to yourself, in the first or second person. Look yourself in the eye in your mirror tomorrow morning and say, "I, (fill in your name), am a beautiful woman, filled with mental and spiritual power." Or, "(your name), you are an assertive woman. You are in control of your life. There is nothing anyone can do to you today to take your peace of mind and confidence away." Repeat whatever you need to hear at least five times—or however many times it takes for you to *feel* it. Hundreds of authors and self-help experts give this advice.

Have Five Best Friends

Have best friends—but not for networking purposes. You need them for emotional support. Your husband, boyfriend, or significant other doesn't count in this case.

Joni Evans, executive vice president and publisher of Random House, attributes her break into the big time to her strong base of close friends. In an article published in *Working Woman*, she recommends having *five* best friends because it's likely that a couple of them won't be available at all the times you need support. Her advice: Be available for your friends and stay in touch with them. Why doesn't a husband count?

> Of course he counts—sometimes. But show me a man who can appreciate fully the panic of a bad haircut just before a boardroom presentation, or the impact of a husband's one-second-too-long look at a younger woman's legs, or our lust for the garage mechanic when we're grown-ups with responsible men, or our dismay at having our period on the night we're leaving for Australia.[3]

Once in a While, Get Away From It All

At the very least, you must drop out of sight one day per season. Take people you love with you, but do not take *anything* from the office: no papers, no problems, no upcoming crises, no personality conflicts, and no people (unless you work with somebody you love—and if that's so, agree not to mention the job). Spend the day doing something very fun, or very relaxing, or very *anything* that strikes your fancy. (By the way, it's even more relaxing if you take a regular work day off to do it.)

Be sure to take your vacation time—preferably in week-long chunks. It's easy to convince yourself that you are so important at work that you just can't be gone for that long at a time. Nonsense! Treat yourself like you would your best friend and give yourself a break. I wouldn't be surprised if week-long vacations add five years to a person's life.

Let Go of the Past

Don't beat yourself up with past mistakes, misfortunes, or unpleasantries. Life is too short—get on with the business of living.

Actually, it's sometimes just as dangerous to dwell on past victories and accomplishments. Remember them—they help keep your confidence high—but concentrate on living in the present. What can you do today to achieve more victories? One thing is almost certain: It won't be exactly what you did yesterday.

Treat Yourself Gently

Finally, be gentle with yourself. Pat yourself on the back for caring enough about yourself to buy this book. Then buy the most nearly homemade cookies you can find and a quart of very cold milk. Go home, put the cookies in the microwave for ten seconds, pour yourself a tall glass of milk, take the cookies out of the microwave, sit down in your favorite chair, and think of three things that you are grateful for today. When you've had your fill, get up from your chair, go to the phone, and call your favorite salon to make an appointment for a manicure. Or take a walk. Or a bath. Or just sit there awhile. Love yourself.

You are a beautiful woman, filled with mental and spiritual power. Treat yourself like the royalty you are.

Endnotes

1. Napoleon Hill, *Think and Grow Rich* (New York: Fawcett Crest, 1960).

2. Phyllis Schneider, "10 Ways You Can Develop an Optimist's Eye," *Working Woman* 13(5) (May 1988): 84.

3. Joni Evans, "The Importance of 5 Best Friends," *Working Woman* 13 (November 1988): 147.

BIBLIOGRAPHY

This bibliography lists by subject the sources mentioned in the text. It is by no means a complete list of all the materials consulted during the writing of this book or of the materials available on any of these topics.

I. PROMOTABILITY

Carroll, Mary Bridgett. *Overworked and Underpaid—How to Go From Being a Low-Paid Secretary to Being a High-Paid Secretary to Having Your Own Secretary.* New York: Fawcett Columbine, 1983.

Catalyst, the staff of. *Upward Mobility—A Comprehensive Career Advancement Plan for Women Determined to Succeed in the Working World.* New York: Holt, Rinehart and Winston, 1981.

Dight, Janet. *Breaking the Secretary Barrier—How to Get Out from Behind the Typewriter and Into a Management Job.* New York: McGraw-Hill, 1986.

Geber, Beverly. "Six-Figure Trainers." *Training: The Magazine of Human Resources Development* 25 (November 1988): 41(5).

Green, Gordon W. *Getting Ahead at Work.* Secaucus, NJ: L. Stuart, 1989.

King, Patricia and Frances Pacheco. *The New Secretary*. Franklin Watts, 1985.

Morrison, Ann M., Randall P. White, Ellen Van Velsor, and the Center for Creative Leadership. *Breaking the Glass Ceiling*. Reading, MA: Addison Wesley, 1987.

Stoltenberg, John. "Turning Problems Into Profits." *Working Woman* 13(5) (May 1988): 63.

II. ON PROFESSIONAL IMAGE

Braiker, Harriet B. "The Etiquette of Office Romance." *Working Woman* 13 (November 1988): 148(4).

Harragan, Betty Lehan. *Games Mother Never Taught You*. New York: Warner, 1978.

Rosch, Leah. "The Professional Image Report: What Matters, What Doesn't." *Working Woman* 13(10) (October 1988): 109.

III. MANAGEMENT SAVVY

Ash, Mary Kay. *Mary Kay on People Management*. New York: Warner, 1984.

Sargent, Alice G. *The Androgynous Manager*. New York: AMACOM, 1981.

Ziglar, Zig. *Top Performance*. Old Tappan, NJ: Fleming H. Revell, 1986.

IV. PERSONAL POWER

Bach, Richard. *Illusions*. New York: Delacorte Press, 1977.

Evans, Joni. "The Importance of 5 Best Friends." *Working Woman* 13 (November 1988): 146(2).

Gunther, Max. *The Luck Factor*. New York: Macmillan, 1977.

Hill, Napoleon. *Think and Grow Rich*. New York: Fawcett Crest, 1960.

Jampolsky, Gerald G. *Love is Letting Go of Fear.* Millbrae, CA: Celestial Arts, 1979.

Rand, Ayn. *Atlas Shrugged*. New York: Random House, 1957.

Schneider, Phyllis. "10 Ways You Can Develop an Optimist's Eye." *Working Woman* 13(5) (May 1988): 84.

Shaevitz, Marjorie Hansen. *The Superwoman Syndrome*. New York: Warner, 1984.

Spock, Benjamin. *Baby and Child Care* (rev. ed.). New York: Hawthorn Books, 1976.

V. GENERAL BUSINESS

Grothe, Mardell and Peter Wylie. *Problem Bosses: Who They Are and How to Deal with Them*. New York: Facts on File, 1987.

Harragan, Betty Lehan. *Knowing the Score: Play-by-Play Directions for Women on the Job*. New York: St. Martin's Press, 1983.

Horton, Thomas R. *What Works for Me (16 CEOs Talk About Their Careers and Commitments)*. New York: Random House, 1986.

Jennings, Diane. *Self-Made Women (Twelve of America's Leading Entrepreneurs Talk About Success, Self-Image, and the Superwoman)*. Dallas: Taylor Publishing, 1987.

LaRouche, Janice and Regina Ryan. *Strategies for Women at Work*. New York: Avon, 1984.

Peters, Tom. *Thriving on Chaos: Handbook for a Management Revolution*. New York: Knopf, 1987.

Quarnstrom, Melody Sharp. *Getting on Top—What Management Won't Tell You When You're Not One of the Boys*. Los Angeles: Price Stern Sloan, 1988.

Yeomans, William N. *1000 Things You Never Learned in Business School*. New York: McGraw-Hill, 1985.

AVAILABLE FROM SKILLPATH PUBLICATIONS

SELF-STUDY SOURCEBOOKS

Climbing the Corporate Ladder: What You Need to Know and Do to Be a Promotable Person *by Barbara Pachter and Marjorie Brody*

Coping With Supervisory Nightmares: 12 Common Nightmares of Leadership and What You Can Do About Them *by Michael and Deborah Singer Dobson*

Defeating Procrastination: 52 Fail-Safe Tips for Keeping Time on Your Side *by Marlene Caroselli, Ed.D.*

Discovering Your Purpose *by Ivy Haley*

Going for the Gold: Winning the Gold Medal for Financial Independence *by Lesley D. Bissett, CFP*

Having Something to Say When You Have to Say Something: The Art of Organizing Your Presentation *by Randy Horn*

Info-Flood: How to Swim in a Sea of Information Without Going Under *by Marlene Caroselli, Ed.D.*

The Innovative Secretary *by Marlene Caroselli, Ed.D.*

Letters & Memos: Just Like That! *by Dave Davies*

Mastering the Art of Communication: Your Keys to Developing a More Effective Personal Style *by Michelle Fairfield Poley*

Organized for Success! 95 Tips for Taking Control of Your Time, Your Space, and Your Life *by Nanci McGraw*

A Passion to Lead! How to Develop Your Natural Leadership Ability *by Michael Plumstead*

P.E.R.S.U.A.D.E.: Communication Strategies That Move People to Action *by Marlene Caroselli, Ed.D.*

Productivity Power: 250 Great Ideas for Being More Productive *by Jim Temme*

Promoting Yourself: 50 Ways to Increase Your Prestige, Power, and Paycheck *by Marlene Caroselli, Ed.D.*

Proof Positive: How to Find Errors Before They Embarrass You *by Karen L. Anderson*

Risk-Taking: 50 Ways to Turn Risks Into Rewards *by Marlene Caroselli, Ed.D. and David Harris*

Speak Up and Stand Out: How to Make Effective Presentations *by Nanci McGraw*

Stress Control: How You Can Find Relief From Life's Daily Stress *by Steve Bell*

The Technical Writer's Guide *by Robert McGraw*

Total Quality Customer Service: How to Make It Your Way of Life *by Jim Temme*

Write It Right! A Guide for Clear and Correct Writing *by Richard Andersen and Helene Hinis*

Your Total Communication Image *by Janet Signe Olson, Ph.D.*

HANDBOOKS

The ABC's of Empowered Teams: Building Blocks for Success *by Mark Towers*

Assert Yourself! Developing Power-Packed Communication Skills to Make Your Points Clearly, Confidently, and Persuasively *by Lisa Contini*

Breaking the Ice: How to Improve Your On-the-Spot Communication Skills *by Deborah Shouse*

The Care and Keeping of Customers: A Treasury of Facts, Tips, and Proven Techniques for Keeping Your Customers Coming BACK! *by Roy Lantz*

Challenging Change: Five Steps for Dealing With Change *by Holly DeForest and Mary Steinberg*

Dynamic Delegation: A Manager's Guide for Active Empowerment *by Mark Towers*

Every Woman's Guide to Career Success *by Denise M. Dudley*

Grammar? No Problem! *by Dave Davies*

Great Openings and Closings: 28 Ways to Launch and Land Your Presentations With Punch, Power, and Pizazz *by Mari Pat Varga*

Hiring and Firing: What Every Manager Needs to Know *by Marlene Caroselli, Ed.D. with Laura Wyeth, Ms.Ed.*

How to Be a More Effective Group Communicator: Finding Your Role and Boosting Your Confidence in Group Situations *by Deborah Shouse*

How to Deal With Difficult People *by Paul Friedman*

Learning to Laugh at Work: The Power of Humor in the Workplace *by Robert McGraw*

Making Your Mark: How to Develop a Personal Marketing Plan for Becoming More Visible and More Appreciated at Work *by Deborah Shouse*

Meetings That Work *by Marlene Caroselli, Ed.D.*

The Mentoring Advantage: How to Help Your Career Soar to New Heights *by Pam Grout*

Minding Your Business Manners: Etiquette Tips for Presenting Yourself Professionally in Every Business Situation *by Marjorie Brody and Barbara Pachter*

Misspeller's Guide *by Joel and Ruth Schroeder*

Motivation in the Workplace: How to Motivate Workers to Peak Performance and Productivity *by Barbara Fielder*

NameTags Plus: Games You Can Play When People Don't Know What to Say *by Deborah Shouse*

Networking: How to Creatively Tap Your People Resources *by Colleen Clarke*

New & Improved! 25 Ways to Be More Creative and More Effective *by Pam Grout*

Power Write! A Practical Guide to Words That Work *by Helene Hinis*

The Power of Positivity: Eighty ways to energize your life *by Joel and Ruth Schroeder*

Putting Anger to Work For You *by Ruth and Joel Schroeder*

Reinventing Your Self: 28 Strategies for Coping With Change *by Mark Towers*

Saying "No" to Negativity: How to Manage Negativity in Yourself, Your Boss, and Your Co-Workers *by Zoie Kaye*

The Supervisor's Guide: The Everyday Guide to Coordinating People and Tasks *by Jerry Brown and Denise Dudley, Ph.D.*

Taking Charge: A Personal Guide to Managing Projects and Priorities *by Michal E. Feder*

Treasure Hunt: 10 Stepping Stones to a New and More Confident You! *by Pam Grout*

A Winning Attitude: How to Develop Your Most Important Asset! *by Michelle Fairfield Poley*

For more information, call 1-800-873-7545.

NOTES

NOTES